In Search of Super Citizens

Published by Clovercroft Publishing, Franklin, Tennessee.

Published in association with Larry Carpenter of Christian Book Services, LLC. www.christianbookservices.com

Cover and Interior Design by Suzanne Lawing

Edited by Alice Sullivan

Illustrated by Daniel Pagan

Printed in the United States of America

978-1-942557-50-0

At age seventeen I starred in national Broadway tours. Then, I stood in the middle of Times Square with my fellow Americans as New York fell to pieces on September 11, 2001.

What amazed me is how we all came together as people and as a country. I was so very proud to be an American! I also became concerned that our next generations might not learn the civics, character, and history lessons that make us strong.

When I moved back home to Birmingham, Alabama, I found my calling. I saw how the Super Citizen Program was transforming children, communities, and our country. I immediately took on the role of "Libby Liberty," and have been touring in my big blue bus, singing songs, and appearing on stages to make sure our children know what it means to have freedom . . . and to be an American.

This book mirrors my real-life journey. I hope it becomes part of yours, too.

Kristen Bowden Sharp

Hi there! My name is Lady Liberty. You might also know me as the Statue of Liberty. But since we're friends, you can call me Libby.

I live in New York City on Liberty Island, next to Ellis Island. I am a symbol of freedom in the United States of America. Where do you live?

Millions of citizens come to visit me every year. I think it would be amazing to visit some of these citizens where they live and see for myself how each one helps to make our country great. My big blue bus is here to carry me across America, and I have an empty seat just for you! Will you join me on the search for Super Citizens?

Get ready for an all-American road trip!

My suitcase is packed with everything I need for this trip. I am bringing American flags, crowns, and books to share with the Super Citizens we meet. I also have plenty of snacks for our journey!

Hop on board and find a seat! The White House will be our first stop.

Libby: Hello, Mister President! My name is Libby Liberty and I'm looking for Super Citizens. Can you help?

President: Yes, I can! As President of the United States of America, I lead our country, sign laws passed by Congress to help the people, and direct our country's armed forces. I am a Super Citizen, but you should meet some research scientists at the Smithsonian Museum. They work everyday to guarantee a bright future for Americans, too.

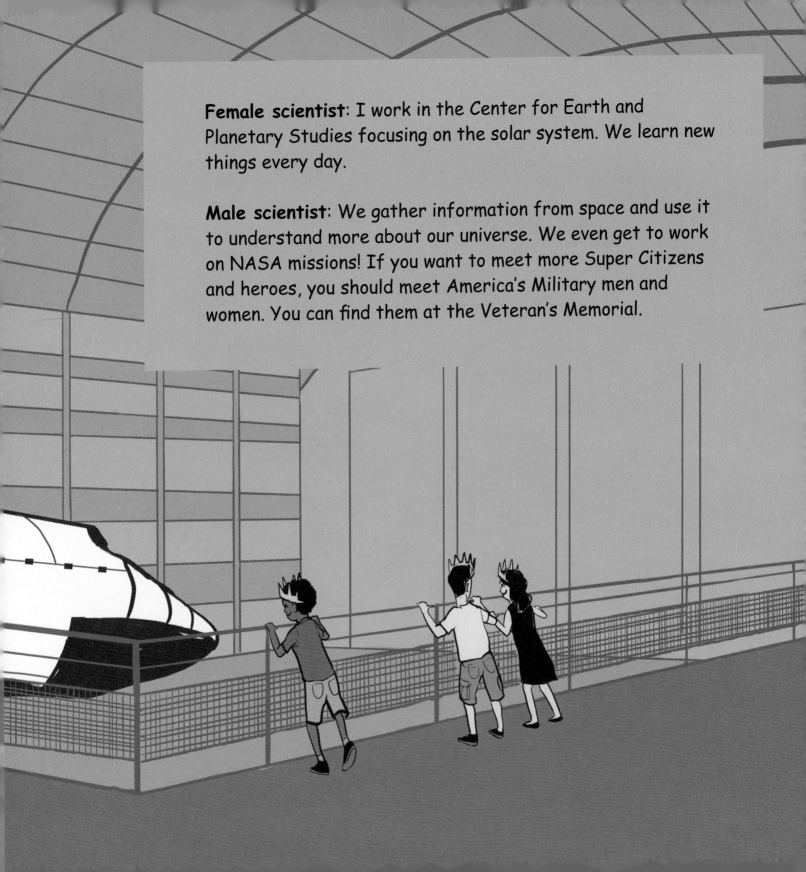

Female scientist: I work in the Center for Earth and Planetary Studies focusing on the solar system. We learn new things every day.

Male scientist: We gather information from space and use it to understand more about our universe. We even get to work on NASA missions! If you want to meet more Super Citizens and heroes, you should meet America's Military men and women. You can find them at the Veteran's Memorial.

Libby: Hello. The Smithsonian scientists told me you were Super Citizens and heroes. What do you do?

Military man: As a member of the military, I keep our country safe from harm. I'm ready to serve whenever they call.

Military woman: I travel to other countries to help people in need and I support our humanitarian efforts in America and around the world.

Military veteran: I proudly served in the military for many years. It was an honor to protect our great nation. We are all Super Citizens, but you should meet the police and firemen who work everyday to protect Americans. You can find them in every town across our great nation.

Libby: Hi! My name is Libby. I just met several members of our great military and they told me you were Super Citizens. Please tell me about what you do.

Fireman: I put out fires and rescue people from harm. I also respond to traffic accidents to make sure everyone is okay. I'm on call 24-7.

Police officer: I protect our city from crime and make sure people obey the laws of the land. Sometimes I work late at night when people are sleeping.

EMT/Ambulance worker: I help people who are hurt and drive them to the hospital. We are all Super Citizens and America is full of people who love and serve their communities.

Wow! You are all Super Citizens! Thank you for your bravery and hard work to keep all of our citizens happy and safe. Do you think American farmers are Super Citizens too? Let's go find one!

Libby: Hi! I'm Libby Liberty. My friends say that you are a Super Citizen. What does a farmer do?

Farmer: I grow crops and raise livestock so Americans can be strong and healthy. Good food is just one part of being healthy. Regular check-ups with your doctor can help keep you healthy, too. The Super Citizens at the Mayo Clinic will tell you more!

Libby: I'm Libby. My farmer friend told me you are Super Citizens. How do you help people?

Doctor: As a doctor, I diagnose diseases and treat my patients when they are sick or injured. We discuss how to prevent sickness with healthy eating, exercise, and attitude.

Nurse: I care for patients when they come to the hospital. I also teach them how to stay healthy when they go home.

X-ray technician: I'm an x-ray technician. I take pictures of the inside of your body to see if you have internal problems. We love caring for people! But you should visit other Super Citizens who live down the street.

Grandfather: I'm a proud grandpa. I teach my grandkids how to be responsible and how to set goals for their future. I take them fishing and camping so they learn to enjoy the outdoors. I also show them how to fix things around the house.

Grandmother: As a loving grandma, I teach my grandkids about the importance of family. I spend quality time with them, reading books and playing games. We bake cookies together, too! You should go to the library down the street and meet Super Citizens who volunteer on Election Day.

Libby: I'm Libby Liberty! I'm looking for people who help their community! What makes you Super Citizens?

Volunteer 1: As a volunteer at the voting booth, I show people where and how to vote. Voting lets citizens decide about the laws and leaders in America.

Volunteer 2: I answer questions and make sure people get a sticker as they leave! Please take a sticker.

Libby: Thank you for my new sticker. I will wear it proudly. I think I'll visit a teacher at the elementary school to find even more Super Citizens!

Teacher: Yes, you have. I am a teacher and it is my responsibility to make sure my students learn important lessons in science, technology, reading, math, and much more. In fact, right now, we are learning American history and how we all play an important role in our country's future, and in the future of our communities.

In fact, I bet you'll find another Super Citizen very soon.

Hey! I found a Super Citizen who looks a lot like ...